What I Saw in
Grand Canyon

Text by Julie Gillum Lue   Photographs by Christopher Cauble

The Exploration of

_____
(Explorer, A.K.A. your name here)

/ / to / /
(Dates of exploration)

RIVERBEND
PUBLISHING

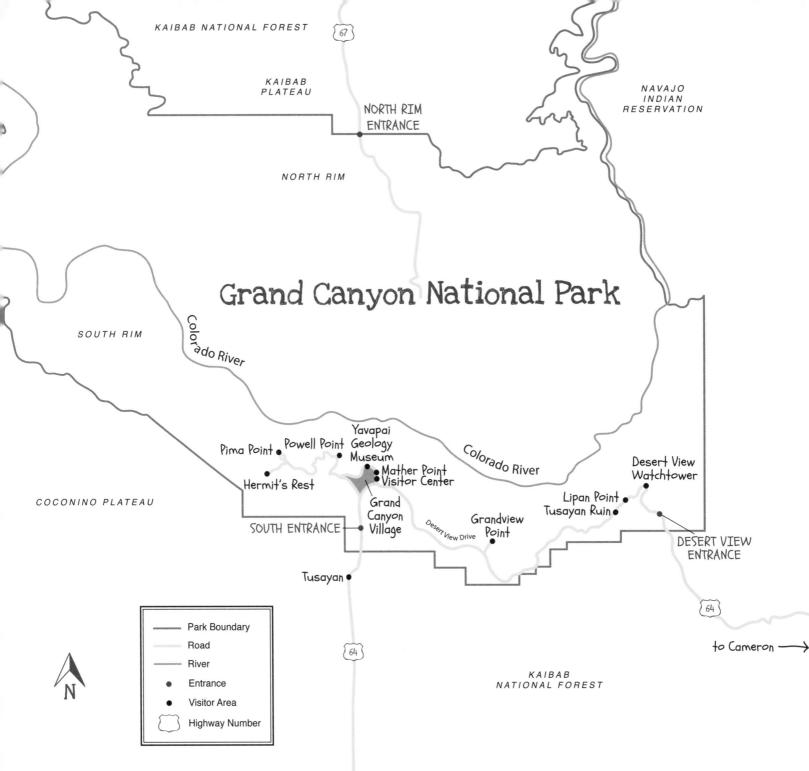

KAIBAB NATIONAL FOREST

KAIBAB PLATEAU

NORTH RIM ENTRANCE

NORTH RIM

NAVAJO INDIAN RESERVATION

Grand Canyon National Park

SOUTH RIM

Colorado River

COCONINO PLATEAU

Pima Point

Powell Point

Yavapai Geology Museum

Mather Point Visitor Center

Colorado River

Desert View Watchtower

Hermit's Rest

Grand Canyon Village

SOUTH ENTRANCE

Desert View Drive

Grandview Point

Lipan Point Tusayan Ruin

DESERT VIEW ENTRANCE

Tusayan

KAIBAB NATIONAL FOREST

to Cameron →

N

	Park Boundary
	Road
	River
●	Entrance
●	Visitor Area
	Highway Number

Contents

Introduction

When you step up to the rim of the Grand Canyon, get ready to start counting. How many times do you hear someone say "wow"? You might even say it yourself. This canyon is huge, at 277 miles long, a mile deep, and about 10 miles wide. Astronauts can easily see it from space.

The Grand Canyon looks complex, but it is basically an enormous example of erosion— something you might understand if you have ever sprayed a pile of sand with a garden hose. Over the ages, thousands of feet of rock were laid down in layers. About six million years ago, the Colorado River started cutting a channel through these layers. The river carved deeper and deeper each year until it reached rocks so hard it could barely scratch them.

To you, the Grand Canyon might look like a different world. For plants and animals, it's many different worlds, from the high, cool forests of the North Rim to the hot, dry desert scrub at the canyon bottom. All these different habitats support a huge variety of creatures, both large and small. They have also helped support people for a long time.

Native Americans and their ancestors have used the Grand Canyon and surrounding area for more than 10,000 years. But few European-Americans had

The Grand Canyon from Lipan Point

seen the canyon before 1869, when Major John Wesley Powell led an expedition down the Colorado River. Reports from Powell and later explorers helped spread the word about the canyon. By the 1890s, prospectors and tourists had started to arrive.

In 1908, President Theodore Roosevelt set aside the Grand Canyon as a national monument. He said it was "one great sight which every American should see." In 1919, the monument became a national park. Now, Grand Canyon National Park protects over 1.2 million acres in Northern Arizona. This year, the park will be visited by millions of people, including you!

What I Saw in Grand Canyon will help you learn about the some of the animals, plants, places, and other things you are most likely to see on the South Rim (which receives about 90 percent of the park's visitors). But if this book included everything you could find, it might weigh more than you do. Some animals, like bighorn sheep, have not made it into the book because they spend most of

Desert View Watchtower

Mule rider

their time deep in the canyon. Others, like ringtails, are nocturnal. This means they are active at night, when you are not.

As you travel through the park, see how many items you can check off in this book. But don't be disappointed if you can't find everything, especially the animals. The park is not a zoo. The animals roam where they please, and many avoid the heat of the day.

While you are exploring, ask your family to help you find answers to these questions:

★ How can you tell if rocks are hard or soft from miles away?

★ What animal can re-grow a missing tail?

★ Where is one of the easiest places for birds to fly across the canyon?

The answers are in this book. But you will also come across things that are not in this book. If you find a plant, animal, or fossil you can't identify, take a picture. Bring it to a visitor center to ask a ranger or visit a bookstore, where you can find books on just about everything related to the park.

Visitor Center

While having fun here, make sure you stay safe. Keep close to your group, and stay behind guardrails and away from unfenced drop-offs. Please read the park pocket map or talk to a ranger for more safety advice.

Here are a few rules you should follow to help protect you, other people, and the park:

★ Don't feed any animals or try to touch them. Stay at least 75 feet from elk, deer, and condors.

★ Don't kick or drop anything over the edge of the canyon. It can hurt hikers below.

★ Leave flowers, plants, rocks, animals, fossils, and historic artifacts where they are.

Your best souvenirs are photos and memories, including the notes you make in this book. As you explore, maybe you'll be able to answer this question:

★ What is your favorite thing in Grand Canyon National Park?

Cliff chipmunk

Mather Point

Like many people, you might see the Grand Canyon for the first time from Mather Point. Does it look as big as you thought it would? The canyon is 277 miles long, about a mile deep, and 10 miles across on average. From Mather Point, you can see only about a third of the canyon's length. But this wonderland of cliffs, spires, and buttes seems to go on forever.

Far below, the Colorado River lies hidden from view. About six million years ago, the river started cutting its path, deeper and deeper, through the rocks that form the canyon. At the same time, the canyon grew wider as rocks collapsed along its edges. Ice and earthquakes broke the rocks loose, and rain and snowmelt washed them down towards the river—sometimes in huge flash floods. The river then carried the dirt and rocks away.

Compared to the canyon, the rocks themselves are very old. The dark bottom layers, called Vishnu Basement Rocks, date back nearly two billion years. The lowest rocks are igneous and metamorphic. Piled on top are mostly sedimentary layers, which get newer towards the top of the canyon walls. The Kaibab Limestone you walk on at Mather Point, at about 270 million years old, is the newest rock of all in the Grand Canyon.

Guess What?
Mather Point is named after Stephen Mather, the first director of the National Park Service. He loved national parks so much he sometimes bought land for the parks with his own money.

☐ I saw the Grand Canyon from Mather Point!

When?

What was it like?

Colorado River

The Colorado River begins as a trickle in the Never Summer Mountains of Colorado. There, it is so small you can jump across it! But in the Grand Canyon, the river averages about 300 feet wide—that's the length of a football field. If the river were a giant faucet, you would need to turn it on for only a couple of seconds to provide a year's worth of water for a family of four.

Without the river, this canyon would not exist. The river carved its own path, a mile deep, and also carried away rocks and dirt that washed down from the rims. All these sediments in the water gave the river even more cutting power. They also gave

The Colorado River from Mohave Point

the water its color, which led to the name "Rio Colorado," or "red river."

Sometimes the river here still looks reddish-brown, when there is a flood in a side canyon. But usually it looks bluish-green. Most of the sediment that would normally flow through the canyon is trapped upstream behind Glen Canyon Dam. Before the dam was built, the river was cold in winter and warm in summer. Sometimes it raged through the canyon in giant floods, and sometimes it ran low and slow. Now, the water is cold year-round and the river flows are controlled.

Even with controlled river flows, the Grand Canyon offers plenty of exciting whitewater. More than 100 rapids challenge boaters in rafts, dories, and kayaks. These rapids have been created mostly by debris flows down side canyons. In a debris flow, flooding creates a thick mud "soup" that carries boulders all the way to the river. These flows, which still happen sometimes, can change rapids dramatically in just a few hours.

Guess What?
Just yards away from yucca and cactus, the river provides a home for riparian (streamside) species like cottonwood trees, beavers, frogs, and herons.

☐ **I saw the Colorado River!**

Where?

When?

What was it like?

Grand Canyon Village

Grand Canyon Village is a town where people live, work, go to school, and share an amazing view with millions of park visitors each year. It's also a historic district with many old, interesting buildings. You may even be staying in one of them.

Kolb Studio

The village was a busy place long before the national park was established. By the 1890s, tourists were traveling here by stagecoach. They pitched their own tents or stayed in tent camps and lodges. Train service arrived in 1901, bringing even more people.

New businesses sprang up to meet the wants and needs of these visitors. John Verkamp built a store to sell curios (another name for souvenirs). Emery and Ellsworth Kolb built a photography studio where people could buy pictures of themselves riding mules into the canyon. The Santa Fe Railway built El Tovar, a luxury hotel. The Fred Harvey company hired architect Mary Colter to design Hopi House, Lookout Studio, and Bright Angel Lodge in the village. These buildings were made with stone and wood to blend with their surroundings.

These buildings still stand today, and parts are open to the public. A peek inside can help you understand what it was like to visit the Grand Canyon in the early 1900s.

Guess what?

For Bright Angel Lodge, Mary Colter designed a "geologic fireplace" using the same rock layers, bottom to top, that are found in the canyon. You can still see it in the lodge's History Room.

Bright Angel Lodge

El Tovar Hotel

☐ I Saw Grand Canyon Village!

When?

What was it like?

Hopi House

Powell Point & Memorial

Where to See it

Along **Hermit Road** (on the Hermit's Rest Shuttle route) about three miles west of **Grand Canyon Village**. From here, consider walking the Rim Trail .3 miles west to Hopi Point for a view of the river.

The stone monument at Powell Point honors Major John Wesley Powell, who led his first expedition down the Colorado River in 1869. At the time, there were no maps of the canyon and the river running through it. Stories told of giant waterfalls, or "underground passages into which boats had passed, never to be seen again." But Powell, a geology professor who had lost an arm in the Civil War, was not discouraged. He set off from Green River, Wyoming, with nine other men and four boats. They floated down the Green River towards the Colorado River, which would eventually carry them through the Grand Canyon.

It was a tough journey. Powell spent as much time as he could studying rocks, fossils, plants, and animals along the way. But the rapids were terrifying and the work was brutal. After losing a boat and much of their food in "Disaster Falls" on the Green River, the men often took their boats through rapids by "lining" them (towing them through on ropes from the shore) or portaging (carrying boats and gear around). Early on, one man said he'd had enough excitement and hiked out. He survived, but three others who left the trip near the end of the Grand Canyon—at a place now called Separation Rapid—did not. Three months and a

thousand miles after setting out, Powell and five other hungry men pulled ashore in two boats. They had made it through the Grand Canyon. Their explorations helped fill in a blank spot on the map and change the way many people thought about this area.

☐ **I saw Powell Point & Memorial!**

When?

What was it like?

Guess What?
The Powell Expedition carried only one lifejacket, for Powell himself.

Where to see it

Along **Hermit Road** (on the Hermit's Rest shuttle route) about six miles west of **Grand Canyon Village**.

Pima Point

At Pima Point, you can see all the way from the rim down to the Colorado River and Hermit Rapid. On quiet days, you may also be able to hear the roar of Granite Rapid, almost 5,000 feet below.

Pima Point is a good place to view the rock layers that make up the canyon (except the Grand Canyon Supergroup). Their stair-step shape is the result of "differential erosion"—another way to say that different kinds of rocks wear down in different ways. Harder rocks resist erosion, but when they break they form cliffs. Softer rocks crumble into slopes.

View from Pima Point

If you learn to identify a few types of rocks, you can watch for them as you travel along the rim. Notice the dark, hard Vishnu rocks along the river, or look higher on the canyon walls for Redwall Limestone, which forms a red wall of sheer cliffs. These cliffs contain many caves, including some used by nesting condors. In Redwall caves, scientists have found many split-twig figurines made by people thousands of years ago, as well as Ice Age fossils of now-extinct species of mountain goats and camels.

Hermit Rapid from Pima Point

☐ I saw the Grand Canyon from Pima Point!

When?

What was it like?

Guess What?

The "hermit" of this area wasn't really a hermit. Louis Boucher was a prospector and guide who lived alone near Dripping Springs and rode a white mule named Calamity Jane.

Desert View Watchtower

Where to See it
About 25 miles east of **Grand Canyon Village** on **Desert View Drive**, just west of the **Desert View Entrance**. It's a paved quarter-mile walk to the tower.

Desert View Watchtower was built in the 1930s as a rest stop for the Fred Harvey Company. Up close, you might spot clues like electric lights that tell you it was built in modern times. But from a distance, this 70-foot-tall tower looks like it could have been here for centuries.

The tower was designed by Mary Colter, who also served as the architect for Hermit's Rest, Phantom Ranch, and several buildings in Grand Canyon Village. While designing the tower, Mary Colter gathered ideas from ancestral Puebloan buildings like the towers at Hovenweep and Mesa Verde. But her final design is not a direct copy of any structure.

Details were very important to Mary Colter. She planned every view and inspected every rock. The tower is built around a steel frame, but she wanted its outer and inner surfaces to look old. To avoid tool marks on the outer walls, workers carefully chose rocks

that were already the right shape and size.

As you climb the 85 steps to the top of the tower, notice the paintings and petroglyphs (designs pecked into rock). The inside of the tower is influenced by art of different Native American cultures in the Southwest. Just up the stairs from the entrance is the Hopi Room, painted by Hopi artist Fred Kabotie. The Grand Canyon is still important to the Hopi people and many other American Indian tribes.

Guess What?
The top of the Desert View Watchtower is the South Rim's highest point, at over 7,500 feet above sea level.

☐ I saw Desert View Watchtower!

When? _____

What was it like? _____
_____
_____
_____
_____

North Rim

Where to see them

If you don't have time to visit the North Rim, you can see it from **overlooks on the South Rim**. It is on the other side of the canyon! The train depot is located in **Grand Canyon Village** just down the steps south of **El Tovar Hotel**.

Grand Canyon Railway

Out of every 100 people who visit Grand Canyon National Park, only about 10 go to the North Rim. Traveling from the South Rim to the North Rim—about 10 miles of flapping and soaring for a hawk—requires a drive of more than 200 miles!

Both rims are made of the same rock layers, but on the North Rim, these layers are about 1,000 feet higher. Because of this, visiting the North Rim feels more like a trip to the mountains, at least until you reach the brink of the canyon. Winters are long and cold, with an average of over 11 feet of snow each year.

The South Rim heard its first train whistle in 1901, when the Santa Fe Railway finished its rail line between Williams, Arizona, and Grand Canyon Village. The train trip cost $3.95 and took only three hours. Before the rail line opened, most visitors took a 65-mile stagecoach ride from Williams. It was dusty, bumpy, took a whole day, and cost $20. Which would you choose, the train or the stagecoach?

The Grand Canyon Railway kept running until 1968, when most visitors were driving their own cars to the canyon. But the railway started up again in 1989, and visitors have learned that a train journey can be part of the fun. Which would you rather ride in, the train or a car?

☐ I saw the North Rim!
☐ I saw the Grand Canyon Railway!

Where?

When?

What was it like?

Guess What?

Each year, about 150,000 people travel to the South Rim by train. The train serves as a giant carpool, reducing traffic on the roads.

Mules

Where to see them

In early morning, mules wait for their riders in a **corral near the Bright Angel Trailhead**, which is west of Kolb Studio along the Rim Trail. At other times of day, you may see them at the **mule barn in Grand Canyon Village**.

At the Grand Canyon, one important form of transportation is powered by hay and hooves. Mules haul equipment, food, and supplies in and out of the canyon. They also carry passengers down the Bright Angel Trail for overnight stays at Phantom Ranch, or on shorter rides along the rim.

A mule's parents belong to two different species: horse and donkey. It inherits some of the best qualities of both, as well as an eye-catching set of ears. Mules are steady, strong, and surefooted.

When you meet mules on a hike, wait on the uphill side of the trail. If you need to move, the wrangler will tell you what to do. Please don't touch the mules or try to feed them. They are working!

Guess What?

Mules have hauled everything from cookies to construction materials in the canyon. If you stay at Phantom Ranch, you can still send postcards "mailed by mule."

☐ **I saw Grand Canyon mules!**

When?

What were they like?

Where to see them

Look in rocks along the south side of the **Rim Trail** where it crosses the **Bright Angel Fault** (about a 10-minute walk west of Bright Angel Trailhead). You can also find fossils in the **Kaibab Limestone exhibit** on the **Trail of Time**.

Fossils

Fossils of ancient plants or animals are found in many of the canyon's rock layers, including limestones, mudstones, siltstones, and sandstones. These rocks are all sedimentary, which means they haven't been changed as much by heat and pressure as other types of rocks. Sedimentary rocks are made of small particles of rocks and minerals stuck together. These particles, deposited by wind or water, blanketed over plants, animals, or footprints—eventually creating countless fossils.

Scientists study fossils to learn what conditions were like when rocks were formed. Some rocks show imprints of ferns or dragonfly wings, or tracks from reptiles or scorpions. Others hold marine fossils, which are the preserved remains of ancient sea creatures. What do these fossils tell you about how this area has changed?

Kaibab Limestone, the rock layer found on both rims, contains many marine fossils. For your best chance at locating them, join a ranger-led fossil walk if you can. You might find fossils of corals, sponges, or clam-like animals called brachiopods (pronounced (BRAY-kee-o-pods). You also may spot some crinoids (KRY-noids), which are sometimes called sea lilies. They look like tiny, pale discs embedded in the rocks.

While searching for fossils, make sure you stay safe and keep off living soil crusts. If you find fossils and want help identifying them, take a picture and show it to a ranger at a visitor center. But please remember that it is against the law to damage or remove any fossils in the park.

☐ I saw fossils!

Where?

When?

How many?

What were they like?

Guess what?

There are no dinosaur fossils in the Grand Canyon, because the rocks here are too old. All the rock layers that could contain dinosaur fossils are missing.

Mule Deer

(Odocoileus hemionus)

Where to see them

Mule deer can be seen almost anywhere on the rim, including the area around **Grand Canyon Village** and **Grand Canyon Visitor Center**. Watch for deer on the roads at night.

Mule deer live along the rims and the river, and sometimes in parts between. They are bigger than white-tailed deer and have short tails with a black tip. Their common name refers to their oversized ears, which look like the ears of a mule. Male mule deer, known as bucks, grow impressive antlers that branch out into forks and then divide again (like factor trees in fourth-grade math).

"Muleys" can gallop at around 40 miles per hour. But when they are startled, they often bounce away with all of their legs springing up and down at the same time, like a four-legged pogo stick: *boing-boing-boing*. This unusual gait, called "stotting," is used to escape danger. In the park, deer have to be alert for predators (animals that want to eat them) like mountain lions. But mountain lions help keep the deer population from growing so big the deer run out of food.

Mule deer eat twigs, shrubs, grasses, and flowering plants. They are more likely to be out feeding at night or during the early morning and late evening. At other times of day, watch for their heart-shaped tracks in soft ground.

You may find the tiny hoofprints of fawns mixed in with those of their mothers, which are known as does. Mule deer does often give birth to twins. Fawns are born without scent and covered with white spots to help them hide.

Guess what?

Mule deer are great jumpers. While stotting, they can cover 15 or 20 feet of ground with a single bound, and they can easily jump fences of six feet or more.

☐ **I saw mule deer!**

Where?

When?

How many?

What were they doing?

Where to see them

Elk are often found near **Grand Canyon Village**, **Grand Canyon Visitor Center**, **Mather Point**, and **Mather Campground**.

Elk

(Cervus elaphus)

If you visit the Grand Canyon in fall, you might hear an elk before you see it. The male elk, called a bull, "bugles" to challenge other bulls and let females know he is available for breeding. The bugle is a loud call that starts low and rises until it ends in a long, high-pitched squeal, often followed by several grunts. If another bull takes up the challenge, they may spar with their heavy, branched antlers. The most dominant bulls will guard groups of female elk from other males.

Like other members of the deer family, the males, called bulls, drop their antlers every winter and start growing them every spring. While a bull's antlers are re-growing, they are covered with "velvet"—a layer of skin and short hairs that is later scraped off. A pair of antlers from a grown bull elk can measure five feet across. Young bulls with skinny, unbranched antlers are called "spike bulls." Female elk, called cows, have no antlers.

Elk are not native to this part of Arizona. Yellowstone elk were brought to the surrounding area in the early 1900s. As their population grew, some elk moved into the park. There are now about 200 elk living on the South Rim, which is much hotter and drier than places they are usually found. Elk often hang around developed areas where they might find water. They can be dangerous, so remember to stay at least 75 feet away.

Guess What?

When bottle-filling stations were first installed at the Grand Canyon, elk learned to turn on the faucets with their noses. Sometimes they wouldn't let people reach the water!

☐ **I saw elk!**

Where?

When?

How many?

What were they doing?

Bull elk

Coyote

(Canis latrans)

Where to see them

Look for coyotes in open areas and along the roads. If you stay overnight in the campgrounds, listen for their howls.

Of the two kinds of wild dogs—coyotes and foxes—that still live in the park, you are more likely to see a coyote. Coyotes are mostly active at night, but sometimes you can find them out hunting during the day, especially when they have hungry pups to feed.

Coyotes prey on mice, ground squirrels, rabbits, lizards, and other small animals. When a coyote sees a mouse, it springs into the air and pounces like a cat. Coyotes also eat eggs, berries, and carrion (dead animals).

An adult coyote is as tall as a medium-sized dog and weighs about 25-35 pounds. Coyotes usually have grayish-brown coats and big, bushy tails. When they run, they carry their tails low, as if they are trying not to attract attention.

In the spring, a coyote mother gives birth to four or more pups in an underground den. Both parents bring food to them until the pups are big enough to travel.

Coyotes can be quiet and stealthy while hunting. But they can also make a lot of noise, especially at night. They bark, yip, yowl, and howl as they call to other pack members and announce their territories. If you hear howling during your visit, you can be fairly sure it is a coyote, not a wolf—the last wolves in the park were killed about a hundred years ago.

Guess What?

You may pronounce this animal's name as a three-syllable word, kyo-O-tee, or with two syllables, KYE-ote.

☐ I saw a coyote!

Where?

When?

What was it doing?

Where to see them

Desert cottontails live in pinyon-juniper forests and sagebrush areas. You may find them along the **Rim Trail**.

Desert Cottontail

(Sylvilagus audubonii)

There are two species of cottontails in the park, and they look almost alike. But the desert cottontail has longer ears with almost no fur inside. The mountain cottontail has shorter, furrier ears. Can you guess which one lives on the South Rim? (Remember, the South Rim is lower and warmer than the North Rim.)

If you guessed the desert cottontail, you're right. The desert cottontail's larger ears work sort of like radiators to help it stay cool. Bigger ears would not help the mountain cottontail, which lives in colder areas like the North Rim.

During hot weather, desert cottontails are more active at night. They

PHOTO BY NPS

spend their days hiding under brush or in the burrows of other animals. In cooler weather, you can find them out during the day, usually in the early morning or late evening. They get most of the water they need from their food and by licking dew off plants.

When cottontails feel threatened, they either freeze or streak off in zig-zag pattern at nearly 20 miles per hour. But many predators are even faster. Desert cottontails survive as a species because they have so many offspring. A female can have four litters a year, with up to four "kits" in each litter. If they live, the young will reach adulthood in three months and be able to have babies of their own.

☐ I saw a desert cottontail!

Where?

When?

What was it doing?

Guess what?

Desert cottontails can climb into juniper trees. They scamper up low, sloping branches.

Abert's Squirrel

(Sciurus aberti)

If you see a grayish squirrel dash up a tree or scamper across your campsite, look closely. It might be a tassel-eared squirrel, one of the Grand Canyon's most famous animals. The tassel-eared squirrels on the South Rim are called Abert's squirrels. They are found in many ponderosa pine forests from Wyoming to Mexico. But a subspecies of Abert's squirrel, called the Kaibab squirrel, lives only on the North Rim and in surrounding areas. You can find it nowhere else on Earth.

In this area, all tassel-eared squirrels have grayish bodies and long ear tufts that make them look a little like rabbits. They also have huge, fluffy tails. But Abert's squirrels on the South Rim have gray tails and white bellies. Kaibab squirrels have white tails and black bellies.

PHOTO BY NPS

During the Ice Age, the canyon was much cooler, and the squirrels' ancestors may have roamed all the way to the bottom. When the climate warmed, they retreated to higher areas on both rims. After many years of isolation, the Kaibab squirrel population began to look different.

If you want to see tassel-eared squirrels, look for stands of big, old ponderosa pines. You may spot a shaggy-looking squirrel nest in the branches. The squirrels eat the seeds from ponderosa cones, as well as the fungi that grow under the trees. They also munch the inner layer of ponderosa twigs to survive each winter.

Guess What?

Tassel-eared squirrels shed their furry ear tufts for summer. But underneath, their ears are still longer than those of other squirrels.

☐ I saw an Abert's Squirrel!

Where?

When?

What was it doing?

Rock Squirrel

Where to see them

Rock squirrels and chipmunks are seen frequently along the **Rim Trail**, at overlooks, and near **Hermit's Rest**.

Cliff Chipmunk

(Otospermophilus variegatus)

Rock squirrels are large ground squirrels with long, furry tails. Their grayish coats are flecked with tan and white. You usually find them scrambling around rocky areas or begging for handouts at overlooks. For your

own safety (and theirs), don't get close to rock squirrels or try to feed them. They will bite!

The rock squirrel eats a wide variety of plant foods—from pine nuts to cactus fruit—and just about any animal smaller than itself. In turn, rock squirrels are eaten by snakes, coyotes, foxes, and hawks.

(Tamias dorsalis)

You'll probably see these little squirrels scampering along the rim or practicing their climbing skills on a rock wall. If they approach you, don't try to touch or feed them. Like many small rodents, chipmunks may bite or carry diseases.

Cliff chipmunks live on both the South Rim and the North Rim, where you can also find Uinta and least chipmunks. All three species are marked with light and dark stripes on their backs and pointy faces. But cliff chipmunks have more reddish-gray fur, and the stripes on their backs look blurry.

Chipmunks eat seeds, nuts, berries, insects, and sometimes eggs or baby birds. When they find food that won't spoil, chipmunks stuff it into their fur-lined cheek pouches to carry back home.

Guess what?

Rock squirrels weigh less than two pounds each, but they have injured so many people they are considered one of the most dangerous animals in the park.

When alarmed, the chipmunk gives a sharp call that sounds like "chip"—a good bet that's how it got its name.

☐ I saw a rock squirrel!
☐ I saw a cliff chipmunk!

Where?
When?
How many?
What were they doing?

Common Raven

(Corvus corax)

At the Grand Canyon, you don't need to look for ravens. They look for you. These large, coal-black birds patrol campgrounds, overlooks, and other places where people gather. Please keep your food and garbage away from them so they can stay wild. If you're not careful, ravens may steal your lunch, scatter your trash, or even snatch your sunglasses.

Ravens are closely related to crows and jays. They look like extra-large crows, except with thicker bills and shaggier neck feathers. Unlike crows, ravens usually fly alone or in pairs, though sometimes they roost in large flocks. Ravens can use their voices to make many noises, including one that sounds like a stick knocking on hollow wood. Their most common call is a raspy croak.

Like crows, ravens are super-smart birds—maybe even as smart as chimpanzees. They use their big brains to help find food and survive in many different kinds of habitats, including mountains, deserts, and cities like Los Angeles. They also use their big brains to play and get into mischief. Ravens can open coolers and unzip zippers to get into packs. Usually they are searching for food, but sometimes they will take non-edible things, like a bag of tent stakes.

If you come across ravens near the canyon rims, watch for an air show. They can do somersaults in the air and even fly upside down.

Guess What?

Eight hundred ravens were once found roosting together below Grandeur Point (along the Rim Trail west of Yavapai Point).

☐ I saw a raven!

Where?

When?

What was it doing?

Where to see them

Steller's jays are often seen near **Grand Canyon Village**, **Mather Campground**, and **Grandview Point**.

Steller's Jay

(Cyanocitta stelleri)

What does a Steller's jay sound like? Almost anything it wants! Steller's jays squawk, rattle, and sing when they "talk" to each other. They also mimic the calls of other animals—even dogs, cats, or chickens. Sometimes a Steller's jay will imitate the call of the red-tailed hawk. This is a scary sound for many birds and other small creatures. With all the competition heading for cover, the jay doesn't have to share its food. If a real hawk enters the forest, a group of Steller's jays may "mob" it and keep up the harassment until the hawk flies away.

Steller's jays are bright blue with black heads and triangle-shaped crests. You are likely to find them in places with pon-derosa pines. These smart birds don't migrate south in the fall, though sometimes they move to lower areas in bad weather. To survive, they collect food during the summer and bury it for the coming winter. They eat almost anything, including pine seeds, insects, fruit, eggs, and baby birds. They watch other birds and squirrels hide food, so they can steal it later.

At the South Rim, you may also see scrub jays or pinyon jays. Listen for large, rowdy flocks of pinyon jays as they travel through the pinyon-juniper woodlands. They are a paler blue than Steller's jays and have no crests on their heads.

☐ I saw a Steller's jay!

Where?

When?

What was it doing?

Guess what?

The feathers of Steller's jays do not contain any blue pigments. The birds look blue because of the way tiny air pockets in their feathers reflect light—something called "structural coloration."

25

White-Throated Swift

where to see them

Watch for swifts below overlooks from March through October. An especially good place to look down (from behind the railing!) is the 3,000-foot drop-off at the **Abyss**.

(Aeronautes saxatalis)

When you stand at an overlook and look down, you'll probably see white-throated swifts—maybe even dozens of them. Listen for their chatter as they zoom and swoop below. These acrobatic, black-and-white birds

ALAMY STOCK PHOTO

spend most of each day on the wing, snatching bugs from the air. They return each evening to cracks and crevices in the cliffs, where they may nest and roost with hundreds of other swifts.

The white-throated swift's scientific name translates to "sky sailor." These birds are designed for life in the air, not on the ground. Most birds have one or two toes on each foot that point backwards. But on a swift's foot, all four toes point forwards. These special toes are

Guess What?

A white-throated swift can eat, drink, and even take a bath while flying.

handy for clinging to cliff faces, but they don't help the swifts stand up. You are unlikely to see swifts perched on anything. In their roosts, they crawl.

As you might guess from their name, swifts are very fast. But no one knows exactly how fast the white-throated swift can fly. Scientists measured the speed of a relative, the common swift, at nearly 70 miles per hour. In flight, the white-throated swift's long, pointy wings flap in a jerky motion, kind of like bats' wings. Its body is shaped like the fuselage (center part) of an airplane.

While watching swifts, you may also see swallows. Violet-green swallows often forage (search for food) in mixed flocks with the swifts. Their flight is smoother and more graceful, and their stronger legs allow them to perch on branches or rocks. Sometimes they nest in rock crevices, but they also nest in cavities (holes) in ponderosa pines or other trees.

☐ I saw white-throated swifts!

Where?

When?

What were they doing?

26

Where to see them

In spring and summer, condors may be seen flying over the canyon or roosting below the rim near **Bright Angel Lodge**. Sometimes condors perch on the "diving board," a rock that juts out over the canyon below **Lookout Studio**.

California Condor

(Gymnogyps californianus)

California condors are very rare. There are only about 80 total in Arizona and Utah, and just over 400 in the world. But when you visit the Grand Canyon, you should still watch for them. Condors nest in caves in the cliffs, and they are often seen soaring over the canyon or perched in trees below the rim.

Condors are huge, black vultures with wings more than nine feet across. They may fly 150 miles each day—at heights up to 15,000 feet—as they search for food. They eat large carrion (dead animals) like deer, elk, bighorn sheep, or cattle. Eating carrion is a messy business, but condors' bald, pinkish-red heads and necks

PHOTO BY NPS

help them stay tidy. After they eat, condors will take a bath or rub their heads and necks clean on plants or rocks.

In the 1980s, many people thought condors were doomed. There were just over 20 left in the world (and none had been seen in Arizona since 1924). Scientists captured all the remaining birds and raised baby condors in captivity until there were enough to release in the wild. Condors are recovering now, but they are still at risk. Sometimes they are poisoned by pieces of lead bullets in animal carcasses.

Condors may be confused with turkey vultures, which are also big, dark birds. But condors have large, triangle-shaped patches of white feathers underneath their black wings. Each condor also wears a number tag. Turkey vultures are smaller and carry their wings in a "V" shape when they fly.

☐ I saw California condors!

Where?

When?

What were they doing?

Guess What?

A pair of condors usually hatches just one egg every other year. Young condors stay with their parents for up to two years.

Plateau Lizard

Where to see them

Watch for plateau lizards in rocky areas, including overlooks, **Hermit's Rest**, and the **Rim Trail**.

(Sceloporus undulatus)

Like all lizards, plateau lizards are cold-blooded. When their bodies are too cold, they crawl onto sunny rocks until they "bake" to the right temperature. When they get too hot, they head for the shade. They avoid extreme cold by hibernating in winter.

A plateau lizard can grow almost as long as a pencil, including its tail. During the breeding season, males show off blue patches at the base of their throats and along the sides of their bellies. You might see a male doing "pushups" on the rocks—he is trying to impress females and scare off competing males. The female buries her eggs in the soil and leaves them forever. When the young lizards hatch, they will take care of themselves.

If a predator grabs the plateau lizard's tail, the tail separates from the lizard's body and wiggles. This distracts the attacker while the lizard escapes. Then the lizard begins to re-grow its tail.

Don't try to catch lizards or grab them by their tails. Re-growing a tail takes time and energy. The replacement tail is also not exactly the same as the original, as it is made of a tube of cartilage, instead of many bones.

While watching for plateau lizards, keep an eye out for other reptiles like gopher snakes or mountain short-horned lizards. These squat lizards, sometimes called horned toads, can discourage enemies by squirting blood from their eyes.

PHOTO BY NPS

Guess what?

In the park, there are more than 40 species of reptiles, including lizards, snakes, and the desert tortoise.

☐ I saw a plateau lizard!

Where?

When?

What was it doing?

Where to see it

Different species of Mormon tea grow from the pinyon-juniper woodlands down to the river. Look for Mormon tea at overlooks, including **Mohave** and **Lipan** points.

Mormon Tea
(Ephedra species)

Mormon tea is a sturdy shrub the color of green olives. It looks like a messy broom growing out of the ground. This plant is a conifer, which means its bears cones, like pine trees do. But you will have to look closely to find them. The tiny cones and small, dark leaves grow at joints along the flexible, greenish-gold branches. Many plants use large, green leaves to convert sunlight into energy (a process called photosynthesis). But with no help from leaves, Mormon tea relies on green stems instead.

Mormon tea plants can live for more than a hundred years. Scientists learned this

after visiting places along the Colorado River that were photographed in the 1880s. They took new pictures and compared how things had changed. After more than a century, many of the same Mormon tea plants were still alive. You can try taking your own photo of Mormon tea in a place that is easy to recognize. In the future, your children, grandchildren, or great-grandchildren may be able to see the same plant.

The plant's common name comes from its use by Mormon settlers, who steeped branches in hot water to make a tonic. These settlers probably learned about the plant's benefits from Native Americans. Many different tribes have used the plant to treat illnesses.

☐ I Saw Mormon tea!

Where?

When?

What was it like?

Guess What?
Some of Mormon tea's relatives are used to make cold medicine.

Ponderosa Pine

(Pinus ponderosa)

Where to see them

Good places to see ponderosas include **Grandview Point**, **Grand Canyon Village**, and **Buggeln Picnic Area**.

Old ponderosas have heavy trunks that can reach over 100 feet tall. They are covered with thick, orange-red or yellowish bark shaped like puzzle pieces. If you find one of these old trees, lean close and take a deep breath. What do you smell? Many people think ponderosa bark smells like vanilla or butterscotch, especially in spring and early summer. Young trees have flaky, dark-gray bark without much of a scent. All ages have long needles, which usually come in bundles of three.

When you walk through the ponderosa forest, watch for tassel-eared squirrels, which build their nests in the branches. Also, listen for the beeping of nut-hatches and the drilling of woodpeckers. Holes in dead or rotting ponderosas make great places to

nest for many types of birds, including violet-green swallows, bluebirds, and creepers.

Fire keeps the forest from getting too shady for ponderosas. Young trees and brush are killed, but old trees often survive. Their thick bark protects them from heat, and they usually have few lower branches to help fire climb into their crowns. But if fires get too hot, even old trees can be killed.

Because ponderosas can live over 600 years, scientists often study their growth rings to learn about the past. They can take core samples without killing the trees. Tree rings tell them about dry and wet seasons and the history of fires in an area.

Guess What?

In this area, ponderosas are sometimes called yellow pines or yellowbellies.

☐ I saw ponderosa pines!

Where?

When?

What were they like?

Where to see them

Pinyon pines can be found almost anywhere on the **South Rim**. They grow down to about 4,000 feet elevation in the canyon.

Pinyon Pine

(Pinus edulis)

Compared to ponderosas, pinyon pines are much smaller and more twisted looking. They live in lower areas that are warmer and drier. The tops of pinyon trees (called crowns) are usually wide and rounded, and their needles are short and slightly curved. For most pinyons in this area, needles grow in bundles of two.

If you find a pinyon pine, look at its base for small, hollow, brown shells. These shells once held pinyon seeds. Every four to seven years, a pinyon tree will produce a heavy crop of cones, with each cone holding 10 to 20 seeds. You may already know how these seeds taste. In grocery

stores and restaurants, they are called "pine nuts." These seeds have been an important food for people for thousands of years.

Pinyon pine seeds are too heavy to fly away on the wind. To spread to new areas, they depend on birds like the pinyon jay. Pinyon jays break open cones, pull out the seeds, and bury them. Later, they return to eat the seeds, but they will leave some behind. These seeds grow into new forests of pinyon pines. Mice, chipmunks, and woodrats (packrats) like to eat pinyon seeds, too, but they don't help plant as many trees.

If you find pinyon pines, look for junipers. These two trees usually grow in the same areas. Pinyon-juniper woodlands are often called "PJ" for short. PJ covers almost 40 million acres in the Southwest, including about a quarter of the park.

☐ I saw pinyon pines!

Where?

When?

What were they like?

Guess what?

A flock of pinyon jays may bury millions of pinyon seeds in a single season.

Utah Juniper

(Juniperus osteosperma)

Juniper trees are evergreens with small, scale-like leaves and shaggy, shredded-looking bark. A tree's bluish "berries" are actually cones that each hold a seed. Try to find a juniper tree you can reach from a trail. Without picking it (or eating it!), sniff one of these berries. Do you think it smells more like food or medicine? People have used juniper berries for both, but now the berries are mostly added to food or drink as a flavoring.

When animals like coyotes, foxes, jackrabbits, and cottontails eat juniper berries, they help carry the seeds away from the parent tree. An animal's stomach digests only the waxy outer coating, while the inner seeds make

it through unharmed. These seeds are left ready to grow in a pile of droppings.

In areas with junipers and pinyon pines, the ground is often covered with a dark, knobby-looking layer. This layer is called a living or biological soil crust (yes, the crust is alive!). It is made of tiny things like algae, fungi, mosses, and lichens. Living soil crust helps absorb rain and keep soil from blowing away. It also provides nutrients for plants. If people walk on the crust, it gets crunched. Even a single footprint may take many years to recover. Staying on trails helps protect these soil crusts and the plants that depend on them.

Guess what?

In a drought, the Utah juniper can shut off the flow of water to some of its branches. These branches die, but the tree survives.

☐ I saw a Utah juniper!

Where?

When?

What was it like?

Utah Agave

(Agave utahensis)

When agave (pronounced ah-GAH-vee) and yucca are blooming, they are easy to tell apart. When they are not, check out their sword-shaped leaves. The edges of agave leaves look like they are rimmed with small shark teeth. The edges of yucca leaves look like they are fraying into strong, white threads.

The agave is often called century plant, but it doesn't live for a hundred years. It stores energy for 15 or 20 years before shooting up a flower stalk. This stalk grows quickly until it reaches its full height—up to 14 feet. Then it bursts into bloom. When the stalk is covered with hundreds of yellow flowers, it looks like a giant tapered candle. After the flowers go to seed, the entire plant dies. You can see these dead stalks and plants as you travel throughout the canyon.

Banana Yucca

(Yucca baccata)

Banana yucca has a similar shape to the agave, but the yucca's flower spikes are much shorter, reaching only four feet tall. When yucca blooms, these spikes are covered with large, cream-colored flowers, possibly tinged with purple. The plant's common name describes its fruits, which look like stubby green bananas.

American Indians used (and sometimes still use) most parts of this plant. Besides eating the yucca's fruit, they made flour from its seeds and soap from its roots. They wove fibers from the leaves to create string, baskets, cloth, and sandals.

☐ **I saw Utah agave!**
☐ **I saw Banana yucca!**

Where?

When?

What was it like?

Guess what?
The tip of a yucca leaf is so sharp it can be used as a needle. Its "thread"—made from some of the plant fibers—is already attached.

Globemallow

(Sphaeralcea species)

Where to see them

Look for globemallow and tufted evening primrose in open areas and along roadsides. These and other flowers may be seen along the **Rim Trail** and in the native plant garden near **El Tovar**.

Globemallows look like smaller version of their hollyhock relatives, but they are much less thirsty. They grow in dry areas in many parts of the park, from the inner canyon up to the rims.

Globemallow flowers bloom on stems about three feet tall. Each flower is made of five orange petals that form a shallow cup around a yellow center. The plants' silvery-green leaves and stems are covered with tiny, star-shaped hairs that help prevent water loss. Don't touch these hairy plants and then touch your eyes—one of globemallow's common names is "sore-eye poppy."

PHOTO BY NPS

Hairy or not, globemallow has been used to treat many different illnesses and injuries. It is an important food for animals, including desert bighorn sheep and desert tortoises. Globemallow has even been found in the dung of ancient ground sloths, which roamed the Grand Canyon more than 10,000 years ago.

Tufted Evening Primrose

(Oenothera cespitosa)

Tufted evening primrose grows from clumps that look like hairy dandelion plants. From a distance, you might mistake its pale blooms for litter along the highway. But up close, each flower is a wonder.

Like smart desert hikers, evening primrose flowers avoid the heat of the day. Buds open in evening, revealing large, white flowers made of heart-shaped petals. The next morning, these fragile flowers fade to pink and die. New buds emerge and the cycle continues.

The flowers attract night-fliers like hawk moths. Hawk moths have the long tongues needed to reach each flower's nectar. Sometimes hummingbirds stop by for a drink, too. They visit evening primrose in the morning before the flowers shrivel into little pink lumps.

☐ **I saw globemallow!**
☐ **I saw evening primrose!**

Where?

When?

What were they like?

Prickly Pear

(Opuntia species)

Where to see them

Prickly pear grows in gravelly places with plenty of sun. Look for it near overlooks, the **Rim Trail**, **Hermit's Rest**, and **Tusayan Ruin**. Paintbrush can be found in sunny spots in forests, along the rim, and below. Watch for it along the **Rim Trail**.

Prickly pear comes in many shapes and sizes, but all species have oval, flattened pads covered with sharp spines.

In spring and early summer, prickly pear blooms yellow, pink, or red. When a bee lands on one of these flowers, the stamens (thin stalks in the middle) give it a "hug" and a good dusting of pollen.

On the South Rim, you can find several species of prickly pear, but cacti are more common in the hot, dry conditions of the canyon. Their thick, waxy coating reduces water loss, and spines help discourage hungry animals. In spite of these defenses, desert bighorn sheep, rock squirrels, peccaries, and humans all eat parts of cactus.

☐ **I saw prickly pear!**
☐ **I saw paintbrush!**

Where?

When?

What were they like?

Paintbrush

(Castilleja species)

Different types of paintbrush grow throughout the Grand Canyon, from the highest elevations to the lowest. All have blossoms that look like artists' brushes dunked in paint. In the park, this "paint" comes in shades of red, orange, or yellow.

A paintbrush's colorful parts are not petals. These parts are called bracts, and they are more like leaves. A paintbrush's true flowers are hidden inside. The flowers, which look like small green tubes, hold nectar to reward hummingbirds and flying insects attracted by the flashy bracts. After pollination, paintbrush produces seeds so tiny it takes hundreds of thousands to make up a single ounce.

Guess What?

Flowers are an important part of the Grand Canyon's ecosystem. They provide food for many animals, from bees to bighorn sheep. Enjoy their beauty, but please don't pick the flowers.

35

I Took a Hike!

Hiking is a great way to get exercise while exploring parts of the park you can't see from the roads. It also gives you a chance to notice small things like butterflies, lizards, and wildflowers. But hiking in the Grand Canyon is serious business.

Many trails lead along cliff edges with no guardrails. Trails below the rim switchback steeply into the canyon, where temperatures get hotter and hotter. Summer storms can bring lightning, flashfloods, and falling rocks.

Before you go, check the weather and read the park's pocket map for safety information. Talk to a ranger if you have questions. Even for a walk on the Rim Trail, bring plenty of water and salty snacks like chips or pretzels. (It can be dangerous to drink too much water without getting enough salt.) In summer, don't hike during the hottest part of the day. If you want to hike a section of trail below the rim, check at the visitor center for current conditions and advice. Remember to bring a detailed map, stay close to your group, and don't hike too far or try to hike to the river and back in one day. An easy trip downhill can trick you into walking farther than you can walk back up.

If your group hasn't hiked before, start with a short walk or two and then decide whether you should try something longer. Here are a few options:

Guess What?

The Grand Canyon has around 358 miles of established trails. The National Park Service maintains 126 miles of them.

Trail of Time

Distance and Location:
1.4-mile one-way walk along the Trail of Time on the Rim Trail.

Use the shuttle bus to begin at Yavapai Geology Museum and walk west to Verkamp's Visitor Center. Give yourself time to enjoy the museum and look down at the Black Bridge across the Colorado River. See and touch samples of canyon rocks along a giant timeline. Don't forget to find fossils in the chunk of Kaibab Limestone. Watch for wildflowers, bluebirds, desert cottontails, and mule deer.

☐ I took a hike!

Where?

How far did you hike?

What did you see?

Monument Creek Vista to Pima Point

Distance and Location: *1.8-mile stretch of Rim Trail you can either walk or bike, also wheelchair accessible.*

This wide, paved trail cuts through a mixed forest with pinyon, juniper, and ponderosa. There are occasional overlooks, but much of the trail is set further back from the edge. This section is less crowded than stretches of Rim Trail near the village. Keep an eye out for wildflowers, cliff chipmunks, and Steller's jays.

Pictograph seen on Bright Angel Trail

Bright Angel Trail (to first switchback)

Distance: *1-mile round-trip*
Location: *Hike down and back up a short section of Bright Angel Trail.*

After you pass through the first tunnel, look up at the cliff face on your left to see reddish-colored American Indian pictographs (paintings on rock). Turn around at the first switchback. After this point, the trail will get steeper and more difficult to climb back up. For a 1.5-mile roundtrip, turn around at the second tunnel.

When mules pass
Stand to the inside of trail
Follow mule guides instructions

I Met a Park Ranger!

Have you ever wondered what it's like to be a ranger? Rangers who work in the national parks are called park rangers, not forest rangers. You usually find them wearing the National Park Service uniform of green pants and a gray shirt with a brown arrowhead patch on the sleeve. Some rangers have very specialized jobs, but others do a bit of everything. Many of them have special training to help people who are sick, hurt, or lost.

The easiest way to meet a ranger is to stop by a visitor center or attend a ranger-led program. Rangers called interpreters or naturalists offer walks, talks, hikes, and campfire programs that help you learn about everything from fossils to condors. Ask about programs specially designed for kids. You can find schedules at visitor centers or on the park's website at www.nps.gov/grca.

While traveling through the park, you may run into other kinds of rangers, too. Law enforcement rangers are like police officers, except that they also manage things like "elk jams"—traffic jams caused when people stop to see elk! Backcountry rangers hike the trails, keep backcountry campsites clean, operate boats on the river, and sometimes help rescue people. The park also has many other employees who do important work like fighting wildfires, maintaining roads and trails, researching the park's plants and animals, taking care of buildings, and protecting historic sites.

You can have fun learning about the park while earning a junior ranger badge or patch. About 30,000 kids are sworn in as Grand Canyon junior rangers each year! Pick up a junior ranger guide at any park visitor center.

☐ I met a park ranger!

Ranger's Autograph:

Where:

When:

More Things I Saw Checklist

Grand Canyon National Park has over 92 species of mammals, 373 species of birds, 57 species of amphibians and reptiles, more than 1,750 species of plants, and so many special places you could not visit them all in a lifetime. Some of them are described in this book, and you may have already checked them off. But here is a checklist of some other animals and places you may see in the park. There is also space for writing about things not in this book. Good luck and have fun!

Mammals
- [ ] Desert bighorn sheep
- [ ] Javelina (collared peccary)
- [ ] Ringtail

Reptiles
- [ ] Short-horned lizard
- [ ] Collared lizard

Places
- [ ] Hermit's Rest
- [ ] "Duck on a Rock"
- [ ] Yavapai Geology Museum

Claret cup cactus

PHOTO BY JULIE LUE

Yavapai Geology Museum

Hermit's Rest

Turkey vulture

Birds
- [ ] Turkey vulture
- [ ] Canyon wren
- [ ] Western bluebird
- [ ] Broad-tailed hummingbird

Plants
- [ ] Claret cup cactus
- [ ] Cliff rose

Other Things I Saw
- [ ] _____
- [ ] _____
- [ ] _____
- [ ] _____
- [ ] _____

Dedication

For Susette and John, who taught me to love the Colorado River, in spite of that flip in Cataract Canyon

Acknowledgments

My thanks to Riverbend Publishing for giving me an excuse to revisit this special place. I would also like to thank Susette Weisheit for sharing many of my trips, including that first hike to the river decades ago, and providing information and advice on the river; and Linda Austin for providing support and ideas on my last visit to the canyon. I am grateful to National Park Service staff who attempt the difficult task of protecting the park while trying to preserve a good experience for millions of people each year.

About the Author

Julie Gillum Lue grew up in the Colorado mountains, where she learned to love the outdoors and public lands. She graduated from the University of Colorado School of Journalism and also studied elementary education. After college, she worked for the National Park Service, US Fish & Wildlife Service, and the US Forest Service. She now lives in Montana, where she writes about family and the outdoors. You may find her online at julielue.com.

★ ★ ★

About the Photographer

Christopher Cauble grew up in Montana, where he began his passion for photography by exploring the mountains with a 35mm film camera passed down from his parents. After graduating from the University of Montana, he became a freelance photographer working mostly in Montana and Yellowstone National Park. His work has been featured in magazines and books, including *Yellowstone: A Land of Wild and Wonder*, *A Montana Journal*, and the popular children's books, *What I Saw In Yellowstone*, *What I Saw in Grand Teton*, and *What I Saw in Glacier*. Cauble is also a nature cinematographer and his videos have been published on many national and international news sites and television programs. He lives in Livingston, Montana. His work can be found at www.chriscauble.co and on social media.

What I Saw in Grand Canyon
© 2018 by Riverbend Publishing
Text by Julie Gillum Lue
Photographs by Christopher Cauble,
www.chriscauble.co
Published by Riverbend Publishing, Helena, Montana
Design by Sarah Cauble, www.sarahcauble.com

ISBN 13: 978-1-60639-108-2

Printed in the United States of America

2 3 4 5 6 7 8 9 0 VP 26 25 24 23 22

Riverbend Publishing
P.O. Box 5833
Helena, MT 59604
1-866-787-2363
www.riverbendpublishing.com